Episode 10

GOOD MORNING.
IT'S A LOVELY, BRISK DAY, ISN'T IT?
NORO (STAGGER)
I'M NOT A MORNING PERSON...
I WANT TO SLEEP FOR A WEEK.
PLEASE LET ME REST.
THAT DOESN'T HAVE ANYTHING TO DO WITH NOT BEING A MORNING PERSON...

THE WORKERS' FOOD?
YES, WELL, MEALS HERE ARE...
...QUITE UNPOPULAR.
WELL, THE FOOD DOESN'T LOOK TERRIBLY GOOD, DOES IT...?

SOME WORKERS SAY THE WATER ALSO TASTES TERRIBLE.
BUT THE QUALITY OF THE WELL WATER IN THEIR VILLAGES ISN'T VERY GOOD TO BEGIN WITH EITHER.
SO IT SEEMS NO ONE HAS NOTICED THE SLIGHT CHANGE IN THE FLAVOR.

SO THEY'VE ALL DRUNK IT?

THIS IS THE RECORD KEEPER'S LIST.
HOW MANY LITERS INGESTED IN HOW MANY HOURS.
HOW MUCH OF THE MEAL SERVED WAS EATEN. IT'S ALL DETAILED HERE.
Cyprien Auclair
21:14
Dominique Balguerie
20:15
22:37
Lucas Guivarch
X
Abel Guivarch
19:37
23:44
Marlin Arnaud
18:53
20:57
Giraud Baschet
X
Vincent Aubin
20:25
23:46
19:07

SURPRISINGLY, THERE ARE A FEW WHO HAVEN'T DINED SINCE LAST NIGHT.
APPARENTLY, SOME BROUGHT ALONG SNACKS...
OF THE HUNDRED NINETY-SIX PEOPLE, THE ONES WHO HAVE TAKEN NEITHER FOOD NOR WATER...

...NUMBER A MERE FOUR.

WE'VE SEEN NO CHANGES IN THE PHYSICAL CONDITION OF THOSE WHO DID EAT AND DRINK YESTERDAY.
THESE FOUR...

I'VE PLACED THEM IN THE SAME DIVISION AT THE WORK-SITE.
THEY ARE SCHEDULED TO BE THE LAST TO DINE THIS MORNING, AT TEN.
THEY ARE?
NOW...

IN CASE OF AN ESCAPE ATTEMPT, I SET GUARDS BOTH INSIDE AND OUT-SIDE THE GATES.
ALSO, TAKING INTO CONSIDER-ATION THE POSSIBILITY THAT THESE FOUR ARE NOT SEED CARRIERS...
...I MADE ARRANGEMENTS FOR A REPLACEMENT GROUP OF WORKERS FROM THE VILLAGES.

YOU'RE QUITE THE WORKER BEE, HMM?
NO.
IT'S SIMPLY THAT YOU RETIRED BEFORE ANYONE ELSE YESTERDAY.
ARE YOU LOOKING TO TAKE MY JOB?

YES.
I DID.

I'LL GO TO THE DINING HALL AT TEN MYSELF.
Cyprien Auclair
21:14
Dominique Bulguerie
20:15
22:37
Lucas Guivarch
Abel Guivarch
19:37
23:44
18:53
20:57
23:57
20:43
00:51
20:25

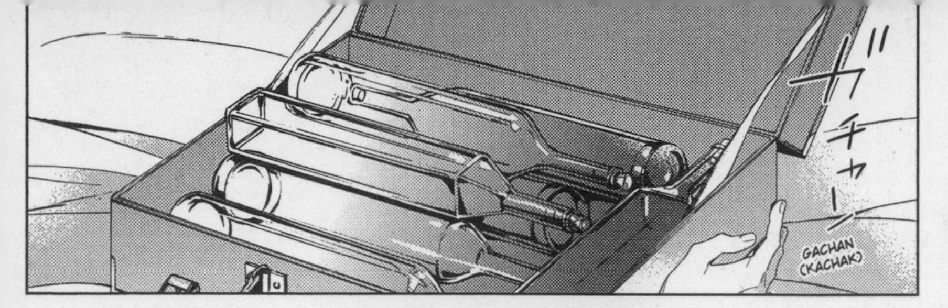

ガチャーン
GACHAN (KACHAK)

HFF!
HFF!
HFF!
HFF!

I'VE BEEN RATIONING THE WATER I BROUGHT PRETTY STRICTLY, BUT I'M ALREADY DOWN TO NOTHING.
THE NIGHTS ARE COLD TOO.
IF I CLOSE MY EYES, I'M NOT SO SURE I'LL WAKE UP AGAIN.
バタン
BATAN (SLAM)
......

AAH.
CAN'T BELIEVE THIS BED'S HARDER THAN THE ONE I GOT AT HOME.
GISHI (KREEK)
I CAN'T SLEEP ON SOMETHIN' LIKE THIS.

UNIT NUMBER FOURTEEN.
BREAKFAST TIME.

OH! THEY REALLY ARE GIVING US TWO SQUARES A DAY.
SHOULD WE SAY YOU'RE NOT FEELING WELL OR SOMETHING?
ボソ
BOSO (WHISPER)
NO, I'LL GO.

BOSO (WHISPER)
IT'D BE BAD IF THEY TRIED TO TAKE A LOOK AT ME OR TOLD ME TO GO TO THE MEDICAL STATION OR SOMETHING...
BETTER NOT TO STICK OUT.

YOU, LIKE...

YOU DON'T LOOK SO GOOD.
THOUGH YOU DIDN'T LOOK SO GOOD TO START WITH.
YOU'RE NOT GONNA COLLAPSE OR ANYTHING?

......
SO TODAY, YOU'RE NOT ANSWERING ME, THEN...

OF COURSE, IF I DON'T TOUCH THE FOOD AT ALL, IT'S GOING TO LOOK PRETTY SUSPICIOUS...

...BUT I DON'T KNOW WHAT'S IN IT.

IT DOESN'T TASTE WEIRD.
I DON'T THINK, BUT...
HA HA HA!

YOU.
I DON'T CARE IF YOU TALK, BUT KEEP TO THE SCHEDULE.
OOOOOKAY.
I'M NOT TOO HUNGRY. I DON'T FEEL MUCH LIKE EATING, Y'KNOW...

......
WHEN I'M DONE, WE CAN SWITCH MY EMPTY PLATE—
WE CAN'T.
THERE ARE WAY TOO MANY PEOPLE WATCHING FOR HOW FEW WORKERS ARE HERE EATING. IT'S NOT NATURAL.
LOOK IN THE CORNER OF THE ROOM.
EVEN THAT GUY'S HERE.
ふあ
FUA (YAWN)

THERE IS DEFINITELY SOMETHING IN THE FOOD.
HFF!
HFF!

BUT.

THE POSSIBILITY THAT THIS IS JUST PURE WATER...
...WITH NOTHING IN IT ISN'T ZERO.

HFF!
NOTHING WEIRD'S HAPPENING TO THE PEOPLE ACTUALLY DRINKING IT.
I REALLY WANT SOME WATER.
HFF!
HFF!

MY THROAT'S SO DRY, IT'S STICKING TOGETHER.
GOKU (GULP)
I'M AT MY LIMIT.

I'LL LOSE MY MIND IF I DON'T DRINK SOMETHING.

SO WHETHER I DRINK THIS OR NOT...

...THE RESULT'S THE SAME EITHER WAY?

ゴくっ！
GOKU (GULP)
！
GATAN (CLATTER)

Episode II

GOKU
(GULP)
GATAN
(CLATTER)
!
ZAWA
(CHATTER)
HEY!
WHAT'S WRONG!?
YOU OKAY!?
ZAWA
ZAWA

GAKU
(SHAKE)
GAKU
GAKU
UNNNH...
GAKU
...!?
HE DOESN'T LOOK GOOD.

UNH ...
UNH ...
HEY!
YOU GOT SOME KIND OF CONDITION?
ZO (SHUDDER)
KOTSU (TAK)
GET BACK.
ALL OF YOU, PLEASE LEAVE THE ROOM IF POSSIBLE.

WHAT...?

ギチ
GICHI (KRK)
ギチ
GICHI
ギチ
GICHI

バチ
BACHI (CRACK)
ワーッ
BUWA (BWAAAN)
バチッ
BACHI
バチ…
BACHI

ヴ
バチ
BACHI
バチ
BACHI

GET DOWN!
NGAAAAAAAH!
ZAAAAAAA (FWSSSSH)
PARIN (SKREEK)
PAN
EEP!
S-SOMETHING'S IN ME—!
ZUKI (THROB)
ZUKIN
ZUKIN
NETTLE?
SO IT WOULD APPEAR.
IT'S NOT THAT POISONOUS.

SO THERE ARE OTHER SEED CARRIERS BESIDES ME?

... OW!
ABEL.
WHAT IS THIS ...?
ズキ
ZUKI
IT'S LIKE ...
LIKE THERE'S A SHARD OF GLASS I CAN'T SEE.
ズキン
ZUKIN

DAMMIT. WE'RE TOO FAR FROM THE DOOR.

—WH...
...AT—
WHAT DID
YOU GIVE
ME?
BIKI (RRK)
BIKI
HFF!
HFF!
HFF!
HFF!

THE
FOOD
...
SO
SOME-
THING
WAS
IN
IT?

DO I HAVE
THAT KIND
OF POWER IN
ME TOO?

NOTHING'S
CHANGED
FROM TWO
YEARS
AGO.
YOU'RE
THE
SAME
OLD
LUCA.

THAT...
...IS NOT A HUMAN BEING.
WHAT DID YOU GIVE ME!?
GUWA (ROAR)
WHY AREN'T THE THORNS WORKING!?
BI (SKRK)
HOW MUCH OF IT DID HE DRINK?
BI
ALMOST THE ENTIRE GLASS.
BI

IT SHOULD START TAKING EFFECT, THEN.
ピッ
BI (SKRK)
WH... Y...?
...YOU ALL...
ビキ
BIKI (RRK)
ビキ
BIKI
ビキ
BIKI
パラ
PARA (FLUTTER)
ビキ
BIKI
UNGH...
UNGH...

HE'S CALMED DOWN...
...MAYBE?

ANYONE INJURED, GO TO THE MEDICAL OFFICE.

IT'S SAFE TO COME OUT NOW.

......

ZUKI
ZAWA (CHATTER)
YOU OKAY?
ZAWA
ZAWA

FINE.
IT JUST SCRAPED ME THE TINIEST BIT.
I CAN'T ACTUALLY SEE THE THORN, THOUGH.
......
THAT'S...
...THE POWER OF A CARRIER...
HFF!

DISTURB-ING...
ANYONE WHO WAS HURT, THOROUGHLY WASH THE AFFECTED AREAS AND COME THIS WAY.
PLEASE TAKE THIS.
WHAT IS IT?
IT'S ALL RIGHT.
IT'S JUST AN ANTIDOTE.

YOU WERE SHOT BY BOTANICAL THORNS.
BUT THEY'RE ALMOST MICROSCOPIC, SO YOU CAN'T ACTUALLY SEE THEM...
THEY EVEN HAVE A ROOM LIKE THIS SET UP IN THIS FACILITY.

THE THORNS HAVE A POISON THAT CAUSES ALLERGIC REACTIONS AND NERVE DAMAGE...
...BUT NOTHING THAT COULD CAUSE DEATH RIGHT AWAY.
I KNOW THEY JUST WENT OUT AND ROUNDED US UP...
...BUT THIS IS ACTUALLY A GOOD WORK ENVIRONMENT?

AH!

WAS ANYONE ELSE INJURED?

BOSO (WHISPER)
LUCA.
?
KUI (JERK)

Médec
Eau purifiée
PURIFIED WATER

!
I WAS HIT.

WHAT ABOUT YOU, HUGUES?
NAH. I WAS SITTIN' PRETTY CLOSE TO THE DOOR, SO I GOT OUT RIGHT AWAY.
WHAT THE HELL WAS THAT, THOUGH?
Y'KNOW? YOU SAW IT, YEAH?
YEAH...

UM...
THE THORNS MIGHT'VE GOTTEN INTO OUR CLOTHES.
WHAT SHOULD WE DO IN THAT CASE...?
YES.
WE'LL CLEAN THEM HERE. WE'VE PREPARED CLOTHES FOR YOU TO CHANGE INTO.

ZAWA (CHATTER)
ZAWA
ZAWA

ARE YOU AND THE OTHER GRAINELIERS ALL RIGHT, NICOLAS?

OUR CLOTHING IS SPECIALLY TREATED...
...SO WE CAN GO INTO THE WOODS OR MOUNTAINS AND OUR SKIN WILL NOT BE DAMAGED BY POISONOUS PLANTS OR SHARP BRANCHES.
OUR GLOVES AND BOOTS ARE PAR-TICULARLY TOUGH.
ちら
CHIRA (GLANCE)
WOW.

FURA (WOBBLE)

WATER...
Médecine f
Eau purifiée

HFF!
HFF!

WHAT'RE YOU DOING?

Episode 12

Médec
Eau purifiée
PURIFIED WATER
WHAT'RE YOU DOING?

AH!

OH, NOTH-ING.
IT'S JUST...
I WAS JUST LOOKING AT ALL THESE UNUSUAL MEDICINES.

MEDI-
CINES?
DO YOU WANT A DRINK OF WATER THAT BADLY?

WE HAD A CARRIER SLIP IN UNEXPECTEDLY, BUT IT'S UNDER CONTROL NOW.
THOSE OF YOU WHO'VE BEEN TREATED, PLEASE RETURN TO WORK.

ちッ
CHI
(TCH)
ぽん
PON
(PAT)
コツ
KOTSU
(TAK)

YOU STAY,
PLEASE.

WHA...?

GIRI (CLENCH)

LET... GO...
GU (TUG)
GU

NGH... WHAT...?
THIS STRENGTH...
DO YOU THINK I'M SUPER-HUMANLY STRONG?
YOU WOULD BE MIS-TAKEN.

YOU'RE SIMPLY TOO WEAK.
YOU CAN'T DO ANYTHING UNLESS YOU TAKE IN SOME WATER.
IF YOU GO ON LIKE THIS, YOU'LL EVENTUALLY DIE.
THIS GUY—!
WE WILL BE CLOSING THE DOOR IMMEDIATELY.
LEAVE NOW.

THAT...
NEVER SEEN THAT BEFORE ...
WHAT WAS IT?
SO CREEPY ...

WAS IT, LIKE, A MONSTER IN HUMAN FORM?

LUCA!
WAIT A MOMENT.
LUCA DOESN'T NEED TREATMENT. I MEAN, HE'S NOT HURT.
IT'S FINE.
YOU LOT, PLEASE GO BACK AND FOLLOW THE ORDERS OF THE OTHER GRAINELIERS.

WAI—
BATAN
(SLAM)
......
ズキ
ZUKI
(THROB)
ズキ
ZUKI
ズキ
ZUKI

LUCA...

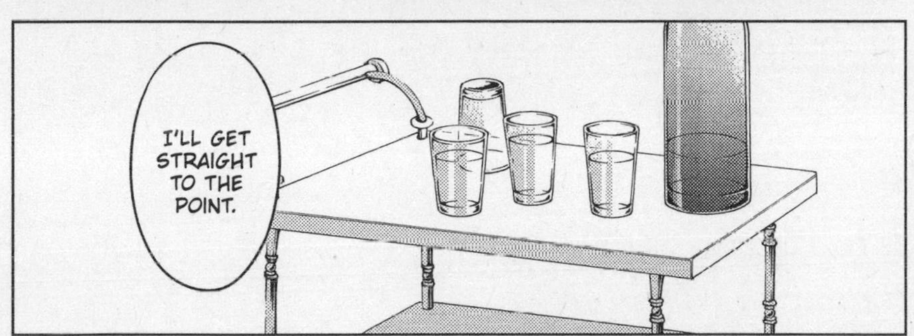
I'LL GET STRAIGHT TO THE POINT.

THE THREE OF YOU LEFT HERE...
...HAVE A CHOICE TO MAKE.
EITHER DRINK THIS WATER OR COME WITH US.

Episode 13
OUR DESTINATION: GRAINELIER HEAD-QUARTERS...
...AND THE INSIDE OF A JAIL CELL.

AND THIS WATER ...
WELL, YOU'VE ALREADY GUESSED THAT PART, HAVEN'T YOU?
IT'S THE SAME WATER THAT MAN DRANK.
IT CONTAINS AN HERBICIDE TO ELIMINATE WEEDS.

FOR PLANTS, IT'S A DEADLY POISON.
BUT IT'S MADE OF NATURAL INGREDIENTS, SO A HUMAN CAN DRINK IT WITHOUT RISK.
PLEASE REST ASSURED.

YOU'RE THE ONLY THREE WHO HAVEN'T HAD A DROP OF WATER SINCE YOU ARRIVED.
YOU'RE ON YOUR GUARD BECAUSE YOU KNOW THIS FACILITY IS WITHIN GRAINELIER JURISDIC-TION.
YOU ARE SUSPECTED OF BEING HARMFUL SEED CARRIERS.
IF YOU CAN DRINK A GLASS OF WATER, I WILL ALLOW YOU TO GO HOME WITH THE OTHER WORKERS.
......
DID YOU...
...LIE TO US?

I DID NOT.
THIS IS INDEED A GRAINELIER FACILITY CURRENTLY UNDER CONSTRUCTION.
AND WE NEED ALL THE YOUNG WORKERS WE CAN GET.
NGH...
I SIMPLY TOOK THE CHANCE TO CONDUCT A SPOT CHECK.
TWO BIRDS, ONE STONE.
BEST NOT TO TRY USING FORCE TO MAKE YOUR WAY OUT OF THIS.
!
IT MIGHT BE A WORK IN PROGRESS, BUT THIS IS STILL OUR NEST, AFTER ALL.
WE HAVE ANY NUMBER OF WAYS TO FIGHT BACK.

YOU LOOK WEAK.
YOU DON'T WANT TO END UP LIKE THAT MAN, DO YOU?
NGH ...
WILL YOU DRINK THE WATER AND DIE HERE?
OR WILL YOU COME WITH US, LIVE A LITTLE LONGER, AT LEAST, AND GO TO JAIL?

CHOOSE.

PHEW!

HMM? HE'S STILL NOT BACK?
OR MAYBE HE'S AT A DIFFERENT POST?

......
...NO IDEA.

LUCA...

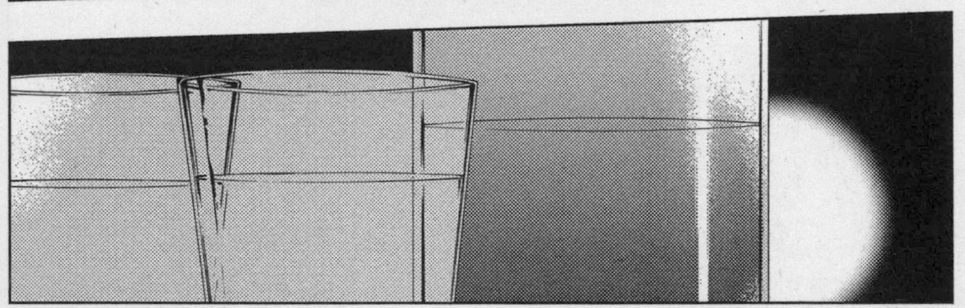

...WELL THEN.
YOU'VE ALL CHOSEN TO BE TAKEN TO HEAD-QUARTERS.
AM I CORRECT IN ASSUMING THAT?

THAT WOULD'VE BEEN MY CHOICE AS WELL.
GASHA (KACHANK)
I'D PREFER IF YOU DIDN'T STRUGGLE POINTLESSLY AND WASTE MY TIME, SO I'LL SAY THIS.
THESE MANACLES WILL NOT BREAK EVEN IF YOU TRANSFORM INTO A PLANT LIKE THE MAN BACK THERE.
THEY WILL JUST DIG DEEPER INTO YOUR FLESH.
JARA (JANGLE)
NOW THEN, PLEASE PUT THE CARRIERS IN SEPARATE CARRIAGES ...
...WITH THREE GUARDS POSTED TO EACH.

I WILL BE FINE ON MY OWN.
YES, SIR.
HFF!
HFF!
HFF!

...CA.
LUCA!
!

HFF!
HFF!
HFF!
HFF!
HOW ...
...DID YOU ...?

HFF...
I ASKED HUGUES ...
HE'S COVERING FOR ME RIGHT NOW...
WHERE IS ABEL GUIVARC'H?
OH! HE SAID HE REALLY HAD TO GO TO THE WASHROOM.
... BUT I DON'T HAVE LONG.
ちら
CHIRA (GLANCE)

HFF...
THANKS FOR EVERYTHING, ABEL.

DO YOU HAVE ANY IDEA...
...HOW MUCH HAVING YOU BY MY SIDE HAS SAVED ME?
HOW MUCH...

EVERY-ONE'S HERE, THEN?
...THE COACH IS LEAVING.
LU—

THIS IS ABSURD ...
THEY SHOULDN'T BE JUDGING YOU, LUCA!

JUST WAIT.
I'M GOING TO BECOME A GRAINELIER AND PROVE YOUR INNOCENCE.

I'LL COME FOR YOU, LUCA.

YOU CAN'T.

JUST FORGET ABOUT ME.
JA (KRNCH)
I'M ALREADY DEAD.
LUCA!
......NGH.

SO IT'S JUST YOU GUARDING ME?

ARE YOU MOCKING ME? YOU THINK I'M WEAK, IS THAT IT?

NO.
THE REASON ...

...IS BECAUSE YOU ARE THE MOST MYSTERIOUS OF THE LOT.

HUH ...?

A HUNCH.
I JUST HAVE A FEELING.
コツ
KOTSU (TAK)
コツ
KOTSU

THERE'S NO NEED TO BE SO CONCERNED. PLEASE GET IN THE CARRIAGE.
I'M EAGER TO GET HOME.

YOU'RE THE
ONE WHO'S
A MYSTERY.

ギッ
GI
(KREE)

ガシャーン
GASHAN
(CLANK)

ガラガラガラ
GARA (RATTLE)
GARA
GARA
ガラ
GARA

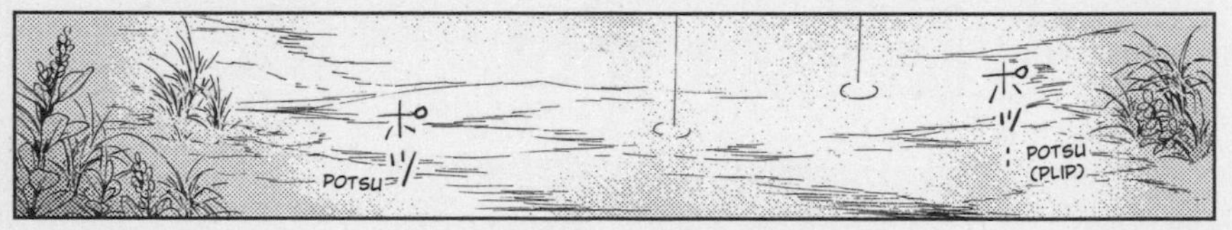
ポツ
POTSU (PLIP)
ポツ
POTSU

ザァァァ
ZAAAAA (PSSSSSH)
ゴトゴト
GOTO (TUNK)
GOTO
ゴトゴト
GOTO
GOTO
ABEL...

NO. THE CARRIER BACK THERE.
ZAAAAA
GOTO
GOTO
GOTO
GOTO

HIM TURNING VIOLENT LIKE THAT WAS NOT PART OF THE PLAN.

MY INTENT WAS TO WEAKEN HIM WITH THE HERBICIDE SO WE COULD COLLECT HIM WITHOUT INCIDENT ONCE HE COLLAPSED ...
A FAIR NUMBER WITNESSED THE WHOLE THING... I WON'T BE ABLE TO USE A RUSE LIKE THIS TO SMOKE OUT CARRIERS AGAIN.
......

BUT CATCHING THREE AT ONCE WAS A SURPRISE.
AT LEAST ONE OF YOU IS LIKELY PART OF A SEED CARRIER COMMUNITY.
THE EXTER-MINATION WILL GO A LOT MORE SMOOTHLY IF YOU SPILL THE DETAILS ON THAT.
YOU TALK A LOT.

YOU'RE TRYING SO HARD TO KEEP YOUR EYES OPEN.
I SIMPLY THOUGHT ENGAGING YOU IN CONVERSATION MIGHT HELP YOU STAY AWAKE.
YOU KNOW, IF YOU SLEEP, IT'LL HOLD THE THIRST IN CHECK A LITTLE.

YOU MUST BE DIZZY, NOT BEING ABLE TO DRINK ANY WATER.

ZAAAAAAA (PSSSSH)

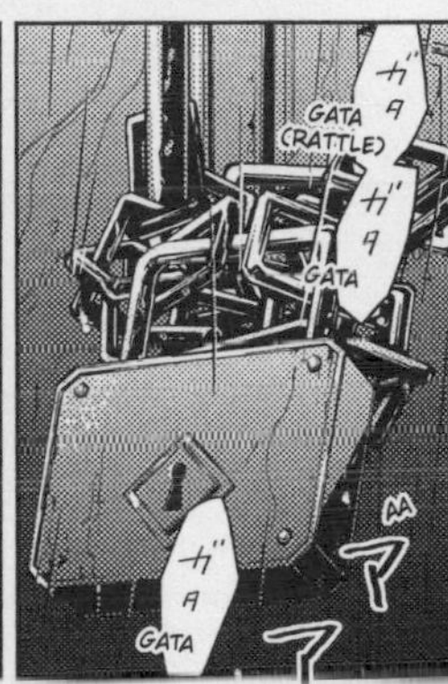
GATA (RATTLE)
GATA
AA
GATA

THERE'S WATER OUTSIDE.
IF ONLY I HAD THE KEY TO THE DOOR...

GATA
GATA
GATA
GATA

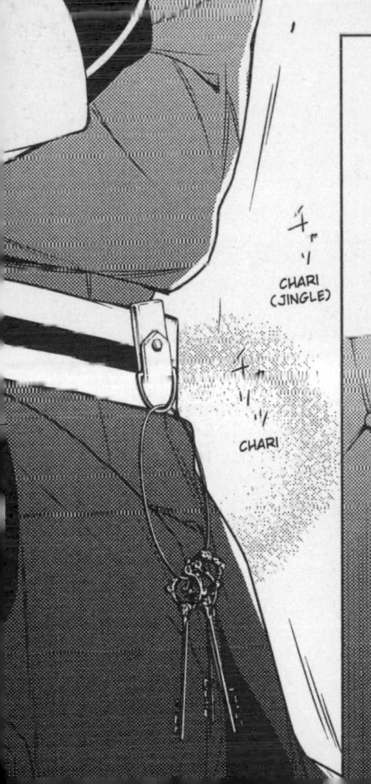
CHARI (JINGLE)
CHARI

ガラ
GARA (RATTLE)
ガラ
GARA
ガラ
GARA
ガラ
GARA
Episode 14

チャリ
CHARI (JINGLE)
チャリッ・・
CHARI

DO YOU STILL THINK YOU HAVE A CHANCE OF ESCAPE?

PLEASE DON'T BE RECK-LESS.
I'LL JUST END UP WITH MORE OVERTIME.
THAT BOY...
ABEL, WAS IT?

IF YOU WERE TO ESCAPE, THAT BOY WOULD HAVE SOME SERIOUS PROBLEMS.
...ACTUALLY, EVEN IF YOU DON'T RUN OFF, HIS PROBLEMS LIKELY STARTED THE MOMENT WE TOOK YOU.
ABEL'S GOT NOTHING TO DO WITH THIS.

...DID YOU KNOW THAT THE OTHER DAY...
...A FLOWER—AMARANTH—BLOOMED BEHIND A CHURCH THAT WAS ESSENTIALLY IN RUINS?
!

NORMALLY, AMARANTH HAS A STALK ABOUT THIRTY CENTIMETERS LONG AND WILL BLOOM ONE OR TWO FLOWERS.
BUT FOR SOME REASON, THIS WAS A FAIRLY LARGE TREE.
THE QUALITY AND TEMPERATURE OF THE SOIL.
THE HUMIDITY.
THE HOURS OF SUNLIGHT.
ANY OF THESE SHOULD HAVE MADE THAT LOCATION UNINHABITABLE FOR THE PLANT.
ALTHOUGH IT HAD WITHERED, IT HAD STILL SET DOWN REAL ROOTS IN THE SOIL...
...SO I CANNOT BELIEVE SOMEONE BROUGHT IN SUCH A LARGE TREE AND PLANTED IT THERE.
IT'S FAR TOO MUCH EFFORT FOR A JOKE. THE WHOLE THING IS A MYSTERY. UTTERLY BAFFLING.

AND VERY INTERESTING.

......
SO?
GOTO (TUNK)
GOTO
GOTO
WHY ARE YOU TELLING ME THIS?

WITNESSES SAID THAT A FEW DAYS BEFORE IT BLOSSOMED, THEY SAW TWO YOUNG MEN COMING AND GOING FROM THE PLACE.
AND YOU'RE SAYING IT WAS US?
SADLY, I HAVE NO PROOF OF THAT.
BUT I DO WONDER AT THE IDEA THAT THE GROUP PERPETRATING SUCH AN UNDERTAKING WOULD SEND JUST TWO PEOPLE TO CARRY IT OUT.

I THINK THAT...
......
...RATHER THAN A GROUP, THE TWO OF THEM ACTED ENTIRELY ALONE.
HAD THAT ABEL FAILED TO PASS THE HERBICIDE INSPECTION, I WOULD PERHAPS BE ABLE TO COME UP WITH OTHER HYPOTHESES, BUT...
...I'M SURE WE'LL LEARN A GREAT NUMBER OF THINGS ONCE WE GET BACK TO HEADQUARTERS AND EXAMINE YOU.
BUT JUST TO BE SAFE, I'LL HAVE SOME PEOPLE LOOK INTO THE BOY AND HIS FAMILY AT A LATER DATE...
...ON THE SUSPICION THAT THEY HID YOU, DESPITE KNOWING YOU WERE A CARRIER.

ガラ
GARA (RATTLE)
ガラ
GARA
ガラ
GARA
ガラ
GARA
ガラ
GARA
ガラ
GARA
ガラ
GARA

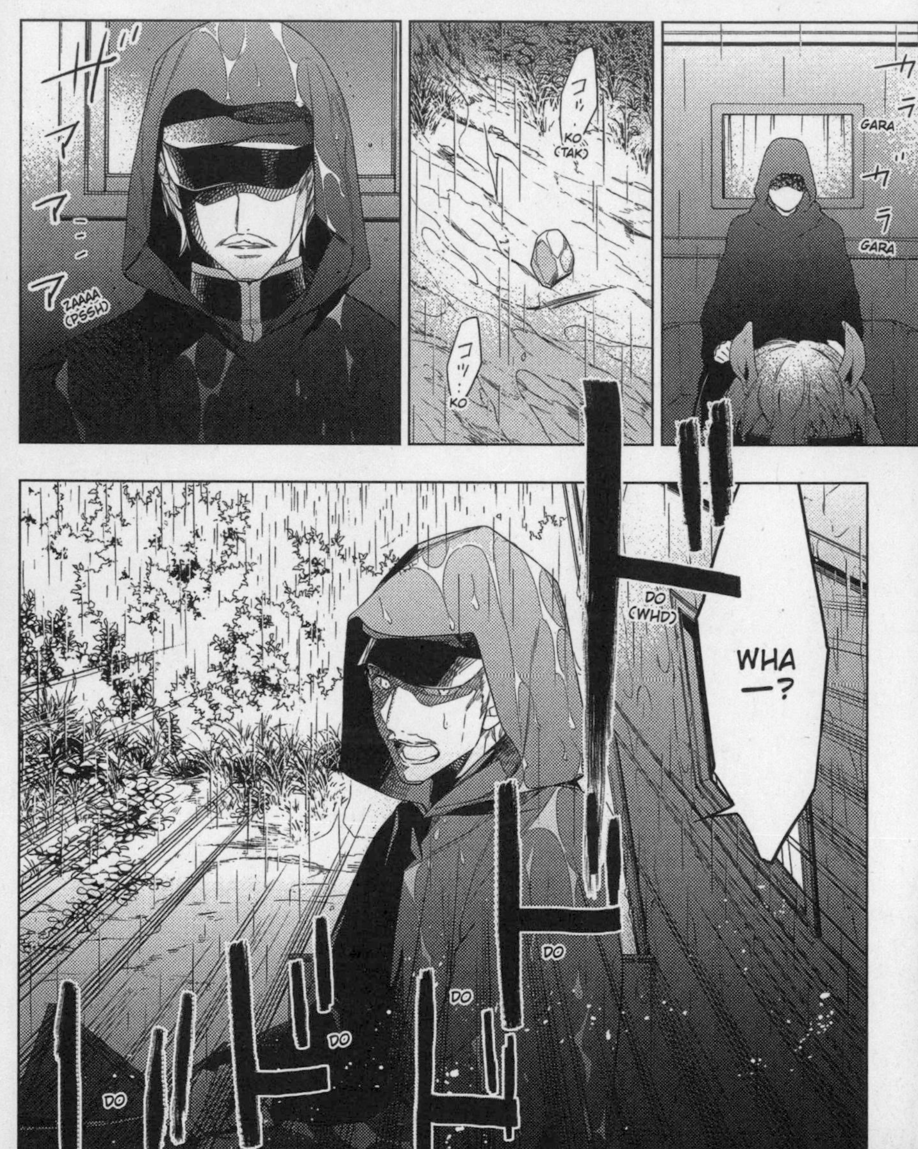
ガラ
GARA
ガラ
GARA
コッ
KO (TAK)
コッ
KO
ザァァ…ア
ZAAAA (PSSH)
ド
DO (WHD)
WHA—?
ドドドド
DO
DO
DO
DO

GISHI (CLANG)
I'M TELLING YOU, ABEL HAS NOTHING TO DO WITH THIS!
AND AS FAR AS ME BEING A CARRIER, ABEL'S FAMILY HAS NOTH—
DO
DO
DO
DO
!
GASHA (KASHRK)

GURA (SHAKE)
GARI (SKRTCH)
GARI
GIIIIII (SKREEEEEE)
DO (WHD)
GASHAN (CLANG)
NGH!
WHAT—!?
......!?
HI (WHINNY)
HII
DOOOO (RRRR)
GARA (KLAK)
GARA
GARA

ザァァァァ
ZAAAAAA
(PSSSSH)

コッ
KO
コッ
KO
(KNOCK)
YOO HOO!

YOU COULDN'T HAVE DIED FROM THAT.
TIME TO WAKE UP.

WHAT HAP-PENED ...?
IT SEEMS THE CARRIAGE HAS FALLEN ON ITS SIDE.
BEFORE IT CAPSIZED, I HEARD THE HORSE WHINNYING OUTSIDE.
SOME-THING'S GONE AWRY OUT THERE.
...IF SOMETHING HAPPENED TO THE GUY OUTSIDE, AREN'T WE LOCKED IN HERE?

THERE ARE CHAINS ON THE OUT-SIDE, AREN'T THERE ?
THAT'S THAT, THEN.
SU (SHF)
THE WINDOW'S NOT BIG ENOUGH FOR A PERSON TO SLIP THROUGH EITHER...
KON (KUNK)

DO
(WHD)
GOO
(KRR)
IT'S DANGEROUS TO LET A CARRIER OUT OF THE CARRIAGE IN THE RAIN, BUT IT CAN'T BE HELPED.
ZAAAA
(PSSSH)

TO BE SAFE, I'LL ATTACH ONE OF THE HANDCUFFS TO MYSELF.

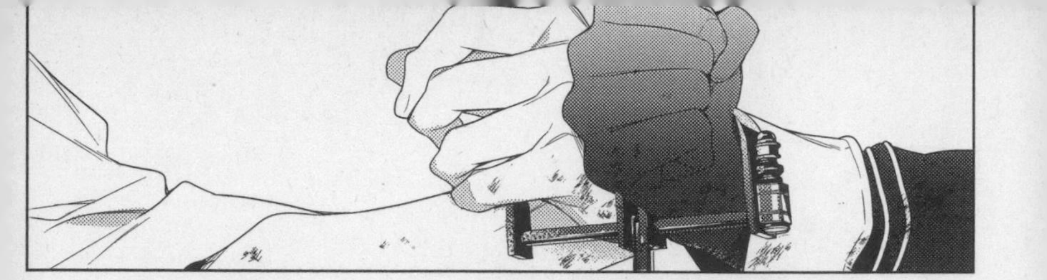

PLEASE STEP ONTO THE BACK OF THAT SEAT AND COME OUT.
YOU'RE QUITE SLOW FOR A CARRIER.
THAT HAS NOTHING TO DO WITH IT.

NGH...

...!

WHAT THE—?

Episode 15

WH
—
WHAT
THE
—?
A LAND-
SLIDE!?

BASHA (SPLSH)
BASHA

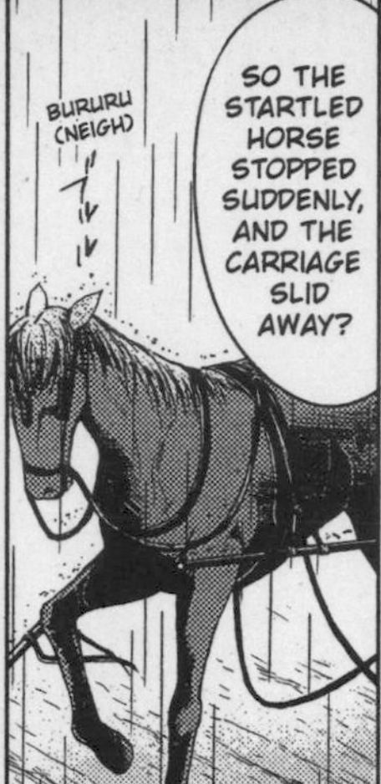
SO THE STARTLED HORSE STOPPED SUDDENLY, AND THE CARRIAGE SLID AWAY?
BURURU (NEIGH)

ZAAA (PSSH)

THE COACHMAN SEEMS TO BE MERELY UNCONSCIOUS. LET'S GET HIM OUT OF THE RAIN.
PLEASE HELP ME.

THE ROAD'S BLOCKED BY THE LANDSLIDE.

BASHA
WHAT ABOUT THE TWO OTHER CARRIAGES AHEAD OF US?

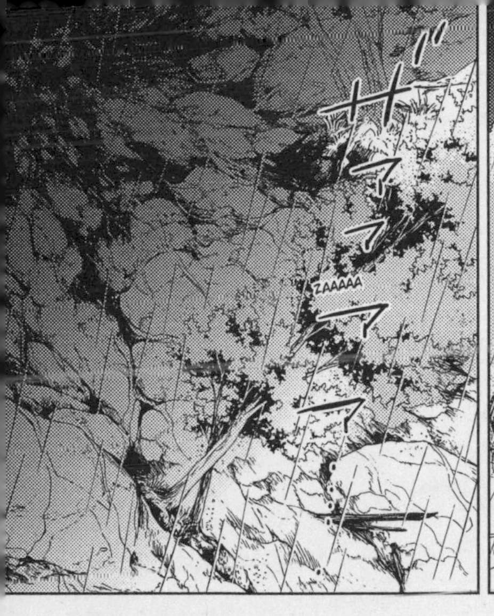
ZAAAAA

...WERE THEY CAUGHT IN THE LANDSLIDE?
THAT SEEMS VERY LIKELY.

......
YOU'RE PRETTY CALM.
EVEN THOUGH YOUR FRIENDS ARE DEAD ...

THEY AREN'T DEAD.
I DON'T CARE WHAT KIND OF TRAINING YOU'VE HAD.
NO ONE COULD BE SWALLOWED UP IN A LANDSLIDE ...
...AND DROPPED FROM THIS HEIGHT AND STILL LIVE.
BUT IN THIS LANDSLIDE...
WAIT. IF YOU WEREN'T HUMAN BUT HAD THE POWER OF A CARRIER LIKE THAT...
...COULD YOU ACTUALLY SURVIVE?

IF I'M A CARRIER TOO...
SAAAA (PSSSH)
...WHY DON'T I HAVE THAT KIND OF POWER?

JARA (CLINK)

LET'S SEE, THEN.
IN THIS RAIN, ANOTHER LANDSLIDE COULD OCCUR AT ANY MOMENT...
...AND THE PEOPLE BELOW LIKELY WON'T LAST UNTIL MORNING.

WHAT ARE WE SUPPOSED TO DO ...?
AAH ...

THANKS TO THE RAIN, I'M BREATHING A LOT EASIER.
HFF!
HFF!

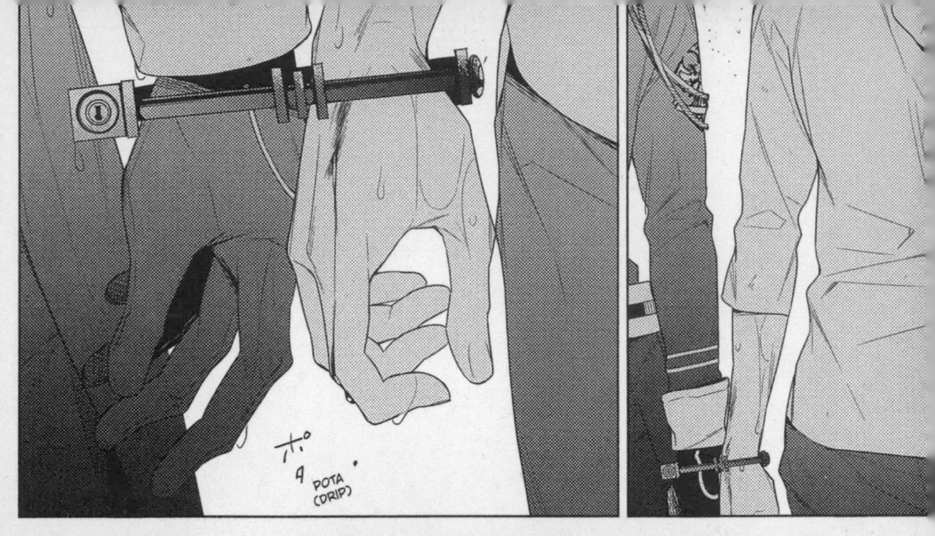
POTA
(DRIP)

SHOULD WE WAIT SOME-WHERE FOR THE RAIN TO STOP?
NO, THAT'LL BE TOO LATE.
WE'RE GOING TO HAVE TO GET DOWN THE MOUNTAIN ON OUR OWN SOMEHOW, AREN'T WE?
WE HAVE TO HELP THE PEOPLE WHO FELL OFF THE CLIFF FIRST.

SO HOW EXACTLY?
OUR CARRIAGE IS IN GOOD SHAPE, BUT THE ROAD IS BLOCKED.
OUR ONLY CHOICE IS TO LEAVE THE CARRIAGE, CLIMB OVER THE LANDSLIDE, AND HEAD DOWN THE MOUNTAIN.
ZAAAA
(PSSSH)

THERE'S NOTHING THIS DEEP IN THE MOUNTAINS BUT YOUR FACILITY, RIGHT?
SEEMS PRETTY UNLIKELY SOMEONE ELSE IS GOING TO COME ALONG IN A CARRIAGE BEFORE MORNI—
BAKI (CRACK)
BAKI

BAKI
WABU (WHOOMPF)

BAKI (CRACK)
BAKI
BAKI
BAKI
BAKI

BAKI
BAKI

THIS—
BAKI
BAKI
BAKI
IT'S THE SAME AS THAT TIME.
THIS IS A SUR-PRISE.
I NEVER DREAMED A CARRIER LIKE THIS COULD REALLY EXIST.

Episode 16

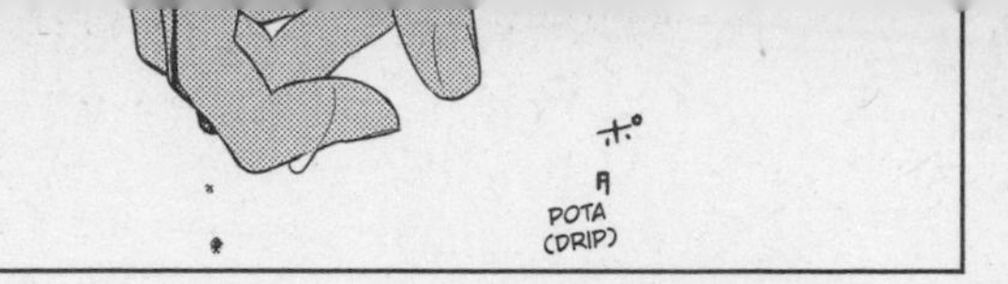
ポタ
POTA
(DRIP)

?
ジ・
JI
(STARE)

PLEASE DON'T HIT ME, HMM?
...?

!?
STOP IT!
BASHI (WHAP)
I TOLD YOU NOT TO HIT ME.
WHAT WAS THAT FOR...?

GYURU (FRRRL)
SO THE CARRIAGES ARE UNDER THE LAND-SLIDE.

YOU...
...THAT.
YOU'RE A CARRIER, AND YET YOU KNOW NOTHING ABOUT YOURSELF.
YOU'RE JUST FULL OF SUR-PRISES, AREN'T YOU?

AS YOU CAN SEE...
...LIKE YOU, I AM A SEED CARRIER.
WHAT?
WHAAAAAAT!?
YOU, THE GRAINELIER RESEARCHER WHO CATCHES AND PUNISHES CARRIERS? A CARRIER!?
SO THEN, YOU—
PLEASE, LET'S SET THIS ASIDE FOR NOW.

FIRST, WE MUST RESCUE THE CARRIAGES BELOW.
BYUOOOO (FWOOORR)

I DON'T HAVE MUCH OF A CHOICE IN THIS SITUATION, SO I DISCLOSE THIS INFORMATION UNDER MY OWN AUTHORITY.
MY SUB-ORDINATES DOWN THERE ARE ALL CARRIERS AS WELL...
...SO THEY ARE MOST LIKELY ALIVE.

AND YOUR ABILITY AS A CARRIER...

...IS STRENGTHENING THE LIFE FORCE OF OTHER PLANTS.

PAKI
(SNAP)
PAKI
PAKI

AND THAT POWER APPEARS TO AFFECT US SEED CARRIERS TOO, SINCE WE HAVE THE SAME NATURE AS PLANTS.
DOKU
(WHMP)

BIKI (CRACK)
HNG... NGH...
BIKI
BIKI

...!?
HEY! YOU!
PLEASE DON'T SPEAK TO ME.

IT'S LIKE THERE'S SOMEONE IN MY HEAD.
HNK ...!
AND THAT SOMEONE'S ABOUT TO TAKE MY CONSCIOUS-NESS AWAY.
BIKI
BIKI
GUWA (WHRRRK)

ZUSHA
(ZZZRRSH)
...NGH!
GURA
(KRRK)
I CAN TELL FOREIGN BLOOD IS COURSING THROUGH MY VEINS.
DOKU
(THUMP)
IT'S LIKE I'M BEING MOVED BY SOME POWERFUL FORCE FROM THE INSIDE...
DOKU
DOKU

UNLESS I CONCENTRATE...
...I'LL CRUSH THE CARRIAGE ITSELF WITH THIS POWER.
DOKU

ZAAA
(PSSH)
ZU
(ZZSH)
ZU
ZU

GOGON (KRRNK)
ZUA (ZSHA)
HNNGH...!
GUN (YANK)
HFF!
HFF!
HFF!
HFF!
HFF!
HFF!
HE REALLY DID PULL THE CARRIAGE UP FROM THE BOTTOM OF THE CLIFF.
HIS FORM AND HIS ABILITIES ARE BOTH DIFFERENT FROM THAT GUY IN THE CAFETERIA.
SO A CARRIER'S POWER CAN BE USED LIKE THIS TOO...

I CAN'T BELIEVE A CARRIAGE EXISTS THAT COULD BE SWALLOWED UP IN A LANDSLIDE AND NOT GET CRUSHED!
HFF!
HFF!
HFF!
THEY'RE CUSTOM-MADE FOR...
...CARRIER...
...TRANSPORT...

GAKU (THUD)
!
HURRY...
OPEN THE CARRIAGE. GET THE PEOPLE...
PATA (PLIP)
PATA
......

Episode 17

!
ガクッ
GAKU (THUD)
HURRY ...
OPEN THE CARRIAGE. GET THE PEOPLE ...

ザァァァァ
ZAAAAAA (PSSSSH)

パタッ
PATA (PLIP)
パタ
PATA
AAAH ...

IF YOU USE EXCESSIVE POWER ...
...IT'S ONLY NATURAL THERE'D BE A PRICE TO PAY.
RIGHT ?
DO (WHUD)
H- HEY!?

WHAT EXACTLY IS THIS!?
THE BLEEDING STOPPED ...

HIS ARM'S BACK TO NORMAL TOO.
HUMAN AGAIN.
AND YOUR ABILITY AS A CARRIER...
...IS STRENGTHENING THE LIFE FORCE OF OTHER PLANTS.

I COULD RUN RIGHT NOW.
JUST GET THIS HANDCUFF OFF AND GO OVER THE LANDSLIDE.

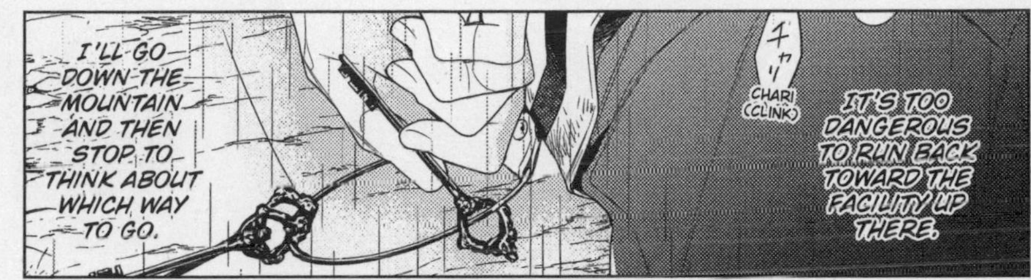
I'LL GO DOWN THE MOUNTAIN AND THEN STOP TO THINK ABOUT WHICH WAY TO GO.
チャリ
CHARI (CLINK)
IT'S TOO DANGEROUS TO RUN BACK TOWARD THE FACILITY UP THERE.

ザアアアア
ZAAAAA (PSSSH)
カチャッ
KACHA (CHAK)

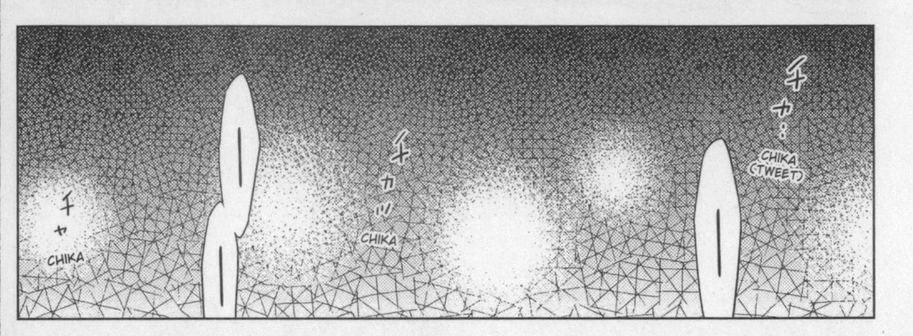
チカ…
CHIKA (TWEET)
チカッ
CHIKA
チャ
CHIKA

OI.
BE CAREFUL WITH HIM.

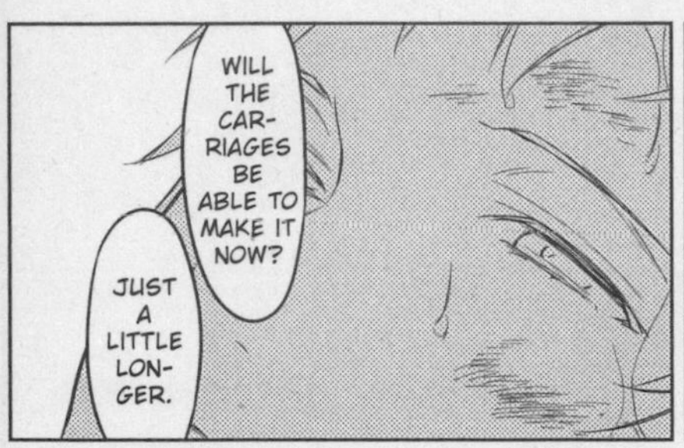
WILL THE CAR-RIAGES BE ABLE TO MAKE IT NOW?
JUST A LITTLE LON-GER.

OH! ARE YOU AWAKE ...!?

GABA (LEAP)
EEP!

WHAT ABOUT THE CARRI-ERS?
L-LORD NICOLAS! YOU CAN'T SIMPLY JUMP UP LIKE THAT!
I'M FINE NOW.
LORD NICO-LAS.
YOU'VE AWAK-ENED?

WHY DIDN'T YOU RUN?

COULD YOU MAKE IT DOWN A PITCH-BLACK MOUNTAIN ROAD IN THE MIDDLE OF A LAND-SLIDE?
I'M IMPRESSED. YOU'RE NOT AS DULL AS I THOUGHT.
... WHAT-EVER.

YOU'RE A CARRIER, AND YET YOU KNOW NOTHING ABOUT YOURSELF.
......
YOU'RE JUST FULL OF SURPRISES, AREN'T YOU?
SO DO YOU MEAN YOU KNOW?
ABOUT ME, I MEAN.

EXACTLY WHAT KIND OF SEED CARRIER I AM.

......
MOST LIKELY ...
...I KNOW JUST A LITTLE MORE THAN YOU DO.

...TAKE ME, THEN. TO YOUR HEAD-QUARTERS.

TELL ME WHAT I AM.

ガラ
GARA (KLAK)
ラ
GARA
ガラ
GARA
ガラ
GARA
ガラ
GARA
GRAINELIERS

THIS IS THEIR RESEARCH FACILITY?

GARA
GARA
GARA

IT'S A PRISON.

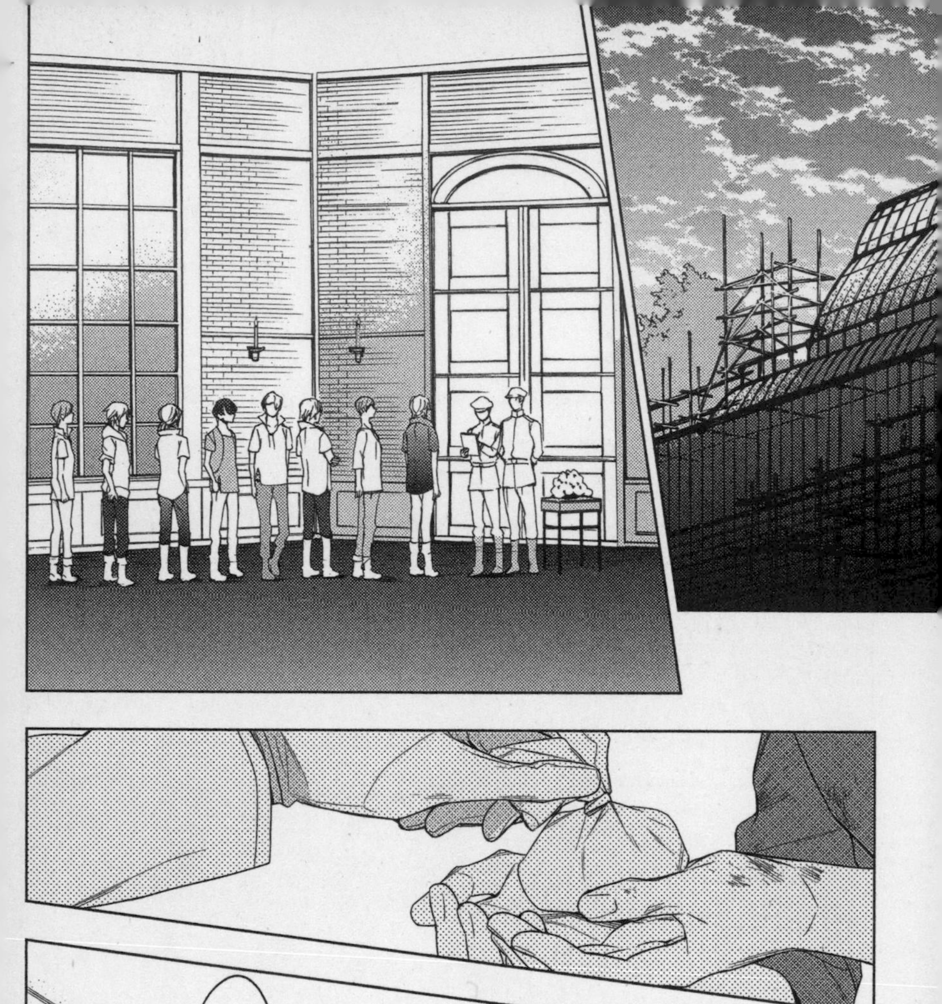

NOW THEN, ONCE YOU HAVE RECEIVED YOUR PAYMENT, PLEASE GET IN ONE OF THE CARRIAGES HOME.
THANK YOU FOR YOUR SER-VICE.
WE APPRECIATE YOUR WORK ON THIS FACILITY.

JARA (KLINK)
I THOUGHT THIS WAS GONNA BE BACKBREAKING WORK, AND NOT ONLY WAS IT NOT, WE GET SEVENTY FRANCS TO BOOT. I CAN'T BELIEVE IT.
I'M TOTALLY SHOWING OFF ONCE I GET BACK TO THE VILLAGE.
ZAWA (CHATTER)
THE FIRST CARRIAGE IS HEADED FOR NONTOUR AND SANTAGNE.
THE SECOND IS BOUND FOR AÏL.
THE THIRD CARRIAGE IS FOR AIGUILLE AND NORTOIS.
ZAWA

ZAWA
CARRIAGES FOR OTHER VILLAGES WILL BE ARRIVING LATER.
I WONDER WHAT THEY DO WITH THE CARRIERS AT HEAD-QUARTERS.

Episode 18

I WONDER WHAT THEY DO WITH THE CARRIERS AT HEADQUARTERS.
THEY WOULDN'T...
IMMEDIATE DEATH PENALTY...
N-NO!
HEY.
ギュ・・
GYU (SQUEEZE)
AT ANY RATE, I'LL GO BACK TO THE VILLAGE—
HUGUES.

HE'S...
...STILL NOT BACK, HUH?
WHAT WAS HIS NAME? LUCA?

YEAH.
MAYBE HE'LL COME HOME LATER IN A DIFFERENT CARRIAGE.
YOU LOOK LIKE YOU'RE GOING TO A FUNERAL OR SOMETHING.
...I DO?
IT'S JUST, WE GREW UP TOGETHER.
I'M A LITTLE WORRIED.

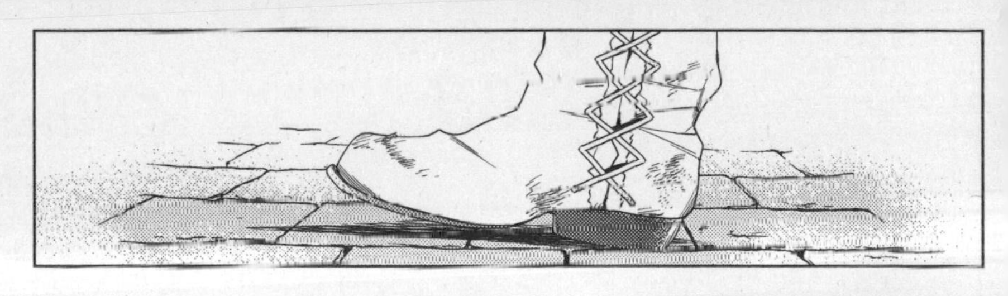

HE GOT TAKEN AWAY BY THOSE GRAINELIER GUYS, DIDN'T HE?

HE'S...
...A CARRIER, RIGHT?

HA-HA! WHAT? A CAR-RIER?
THE POWER THAT CAUSED ALL THE COMMOTION IN THE CAFETERIA? IN LUCA?
WHY...
...ARE YOU ...?

WHO EXACTLY ARE YOU?

WE CAN'T TALK HERE.
WHEN WE GET IN THE CARRIAGE HOME...
...WE'LL BOTH GET OUT AT MY VILLAGE.
BUT...
...I HAVE TO GO BACK TO MY VILLAGE AND TELL MY FAMILY ABOUT
MOST LIKELY...
...GRAINELIERS ARE ALREADY ON THEIR WAY TO YOUR HOUSE, GIVEN THAT YOU WERE HIDING A CARRIER.
THEY MIGHT ALREADY BE INTERROGATING YOUR FATHER OR BRINGING HIM INTO THEIR HEAD-QUARTERS.
THEN...
...ALL THE MORE REASON FOR ME TO GO HOME!

YOU CAN'T DO ANYTHING BY YOURSELF.
EVEN SO!
MY DAD, LUCA...
I'M ALL THEY HAVE.
I HAVE TO HELP THEM.
AND ME TOO.

DAD AND LUCA ARE ALL I HAVE.
AND I MADE A PROMISE.

ANYONE STILL WAITING TO BOARD GET THE COACHES?
TRUST ME. GET OUT OF THE CARRIAGE MIDWAY.
I WON'T SAY FOR SURE WE'LL SAVE THEM...
...BUT I'LL HELP YOU.

WHAT?
HEY!
HUGUES!
BATA (RATTLE)
BATA

Episode 19

GATA (RATTLE)
GATA
GATA
GATA

GATA
GAKON (CLUNK)
GATA
GATA
GATA

CAN I REALLY TRUST HIM?

BUT IT'S JUST LIKE HE SAID...
NOT ONLY HAS LUCA BEEN CAUGHT BY THE GRAINELIERS, BUT THERE'S A GOOD CHANCE THEY'VE GONE TO MY HOUSE TO INVESTIGATE TOO...

GATA
IT'S RISKY TO JUST BLINDLY TRUST HIM...
HE'S KNOWS MY WEAK POINT WITH THE WHOLE THING WITH LUCA.
MAYBE HE'S PLANNING TO BLACKMAIL ME.
GATA

GYU (SQUEEZE)
AND IF THEY'VE GOT DAD, THEN...
...I'M THE ONLY ONE LEFT TO HELP EITHER OF THEM.
I DON'T HAVE A CHOICE.
HUGUES.
I'LL GET OUT WITH YOU.

GATA
GATA
GATA
GATA

THE VILLAGE OF AIGUILLE.
ギィィ…
GIII (KREEE)

ANYONE WHO RODE FROM THIS VILLAGE, GET OUT HERE.
ザワ
ZAWA (CHATTER)
ザワ
ZAWA
ザワ
ZAWA
ザッ
ZA (KSH)

パラ
PARA (FLIP)

BLACK SHIRT, GRAY HAIR.
BLUE JACKET, BLOND.

HUGUES BALBASTRE AND FLORENT LASALLE, YES?
MM-HMM.
THANK YOU FOR YOUR HARD WORK.
YOU MAY GO.

WE MADE IT!
TA (TAK)

THAT FLUNKEY'S CHECK WASN'T MUCH OF A CHECK.
ガラ GARA (RATTLE)
ガラ GARA
ガラ GARA
たっ TA (TAK)
たっ TA
UM...
IS THIS REALLY OKAY?
LOOK. THE CARRIAGE IS GONE ALREADY.
たっ TA

NOT THAT. YOUR FRIEND WHO'S STILL IN IT IN MY PLACE.
ガタ GATA (SHAKE)
ガタ GATA
WON'T THEY DO TERRIBLE THINGS TO HIM IF THEY FIND OUT HE'S A FAKE?
ガタ GATA
HE'S FLEET OF FOOT IF NOTHING ELSE. HE'LL BE FINE.
AND HE'S A CARRIER TOO.
!

IN THIS WORLD...
...THERE ARE PROBABLY A LOT MORE SEED CARRIERS THAN YOU GUYS THOUGHT, Y'KNOW?

HYOU (HYOO)

THAT'S THE LOOKOUT.

ギィイ・・
GIII
(KREE)

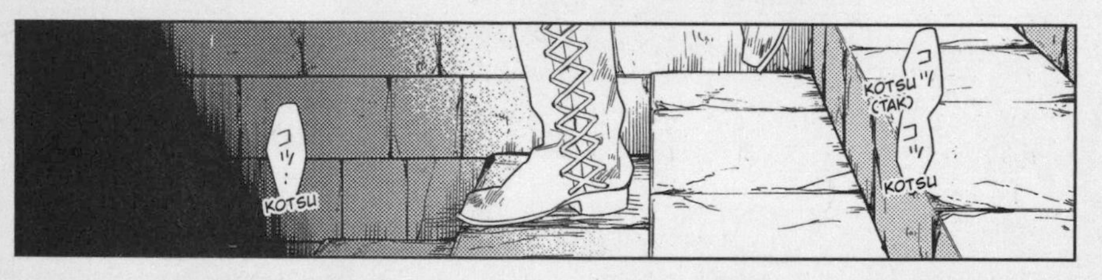
コツ
KOTSU
(TAK)
コツ
KOTSU
コツ・・
KOTSU

コツ
KOTSU
コツ
KOTSU
コツ
KOTSU
WELL, YOU'RE BACK SOONER THAN I EXPECTED, HUGUES.
KA
(KLAK)

WHAT ABOUT LASALLE?
WE'VE GOT A LITTLE SITUATION, SO HE'S TAKING A DIFFERENT ROUTE HOME.
THIS COULD TAKE A WHILE. LET'S TALK INSIDE.
チカッ
CHIKA (FWWK)
!
NO.
TALK HERE.
YOU STILL HAVEN'T TOLD ME WHO THIS GUY IS.

Episode 20

WHY ARE YOU WEARING LASALLE'S CLOTHES?
AND DOES YOU COMING HERE MEAN YOU'RE ALSO...?
NO.
HE'S A NORMAL HUMAN.
BUT HIS BEST FRIEND'S A CARRIER WHO WAS TAKEN AWAY BY THE GRAINELIERS.

......
YOU'RE SAYING HE'S JOINING US?
I WAS GOING TO ASK HIM THAT NOW. THAT'S WHY I BROUGHT HIM.
OI...

I COULDN'T EXPLAIN THINGS WHILE WE WERE BEING WATCHED BY GRAINELIERS...
...BUT...
...HE'LL PROBABLY JOIN US.

... HUGUES.
WHAT IS THIS PLACE?

I WANT TO ASK YOU SOMETHING FIRST.

ARE YOU READY?

FOR THE SAKE OF YOUR FRIEND...
...AND YOUR FATHER...
...ARE YOU READY TO SACRIFICE EVEN YOURSELF IF YOU NEED TO?

......
......YES.

I CAN'T JUST RUN AWAY BY MYSELF.

IF ANY-THING HAPPENS, HUGUES...
...IT'S ALL ON YOU.
I KNOW. GOT IT.

GACHA (KACHAK)
ガチャッ
ザワッ…
ZAWA (MURMUR)

THIS IS AN INSECTE OFFICE.
IT'S MORE HIDEOUT THAN SAFE HOUSE, THOUGH. IT'S PRETTY ROUGH.

INSECTE?

ANTI-GRAINELIER FORCES.

!?
SO THEN, THAT MEANS ...
TO THE WORLD AT LARGE, WE'RE SOMETHING LIKE A TERRORIST GROUP.
T-TER-RORIST?
THE GRAINELIERS DON'T JUST STUDY SEEDS. AREN'T THEY ALSO A NATIONAL RESEARCH INSTITUTE CHARGED WITH PUBLIC SAFETY AND TAKING CARE OF CITIZENS?
WHY DO YOU HAVE TO ATTACK THEM?

BECAUSE ...
...THE RESEARCH THE GRAINELIERS HAVE BEEN DESPERATELY AND DILIGENTLY WORKING ON ALL THESE YEARS IS ITSELF THE PROBLEM.
THE RESEARCH ... IS THE PROBLEM?

WE HAVE CONVICTIONS. AND EVERYONE IN INSECTE AGREES WITH THOSE CONVICTIONS.
YOU'RE BLABBING WAY TOO MUCH TO SOMEONE WHO'S NOT ONE OF US, HUGUES.

WE DON'T KNOW WHETHER OR NOT YOU'LL SAY SOMETHING SOMEWHERE IF YOU DON'T JOIN US AND LEAVE THIS PLACE...
...AND THEN THE GRAINELIERS WILL GET WIND OF IT.

AND THE IDEA THAT YOU'RE A SPY ISN'T OUT OF THE QUESTION EITHER.
YOU'LL HEAR THE REST OF THIS STORY ONCE YOU PROVE YOUR RESOLVE TO JOIN US.
......
HUGUES, WHY DID YOU BRING ME HERE?
I MEAN, UP TO NOW, THE GRAINELIERS HAVE BEEN ALMOST GODLIKE TO THE PEOPLE...
TO BE HONEST...
...YOU SPRINGING ALL THIS ON ME...
I HAVE NO IDEA HOW MUCH IS TRUE OR HOW MUCH I CAN TRUST YOU.
AND...
AND...
...I JUST WANT TO SAVE LUCA AND MY DAD.
I'M NO HERO OF THE PEOPLE.

GATA (CLATTER)
YEAH, FAIR ENOUGH.
BUT I'LL ASK ANYWAY. JOIN US, ABEL.
IN EXCHANGE, WE'LL GIVE YOU "POSSIBILITY."
THE POSSIBILITY OF THE SEED CARRIER. THE POSSIBILITY OF INCREDIBLE POWER.

WITH THIS POWER, YOU CAN PROTECT THAT CARRIER AND YOUR FATHER.
PUT ANOTHER WAY, WITHOUT THE POWER, YOU'RE GARBAGE.

THE SPECIAL RESEARCHER GRAINELIER DIVISION IS FULL OF CARRIERS.

THEY CAN'T BE!?
THEY TALK ABOUT HOW HAVING A SEED IN THE BODY IS ILLEGAL, HOW IT MAKES YOU A MONSTER.
BUT ALL THE WHILE, THEY USE THOSE MONSTERS TO HUNT MONSTERS.
THEY'RE NOT SCIENTISTS.
THEY'RE SOLDIERS.

OTHER SEED CARRIERS ARE THE ONLY ONES WHO CAN GO UP AGAINST THESE SPECIAL RESEARCHERS.
AND ONLY THOSE WITH A HIGH LEVEL OF COMPATIBILITY BETWEEN SEED AND BODY.
THOSE SUITED FOR WAR.

BUT THE SURVIVAL RATE FOR PEOPLE WHO SWALLOW SEEDS IS—
HERE...
...WE WELCOME ANYONE WHO WISHES TO JOIN US.
BUT...
...ONLY THOSE WHO SWALLOW A SEED AND SURVIVE.
2.8%.

IN OTHER WORDS ....
...YOU'RE TELLING ME TO EAT A POISON SEED?

WITH A 97% CHANCE I'LL DIE...
... THERE'S NO POINT.
IF I DIE, WHO'S THERE FOR LUCA?
I'M NOT TELLING YOU TO TAKE JUST ANY SEED.
WE HAVE DATA. WE'VE STUDIED HARMFUL SEEDS ON OUR OWN FOR MANY YEARS.
HUMANS HAVE AFFINITIES.
SOME SEEDS ARE MORE OR LESS COMPAT-IBLE.

WE DO SOME TESTS AND NARROW IT DOWN TO ONE SEED YOU'RE COMPATIBLE WITH. YOU TAKE THAT.
JUST ONE?
THE BODY CAN'T HANDLE THE CELLULAR FUSION OF THE SEEDS TOGETHER WHEN YOU TAKE TWO OR MORE SEEDS. YOU DIE.
VERY, VERY RARELY ...

...THERE ARE PEOPLE WHO TAKE SEVERAL SEEDS AND STILL DON'T DIE. BUT IT'S BEST NOT TO PIN YOUR HOPES ON THAT.

EVEN WITH ALL THE TESTING, THOUGH ...
...IF WE GET THE FATALITY RATE DOWN TO 60%, WE'RE DOING PRETTY GOOD.
60%
97.2%
THAT'S A LOT BETTER THAN 97%, RIGHT?

BUT WHEN YOU TAKE A SEED, SOME SIDE EFFECTS ARE INEVITABLE. THEY HAPPEN IN EVERYONE.

......
I DON'T KNOW WHAT THE GRAINELIERS DO IN THEIR LABS...
...BUT I BELIEVE ...
...WHAT YOU'RE SAYING, HUGUES.

YOU DON'T SEEM LIKE YOU'RE LYING.
AND YOU PROBABLY DON'T GET ANYTHING OUT OF LYING TO ME.
BUT...

I CAN'T RIGHT NOW.
I CAN'T ...
...DIE JUST YET.

...I SEE...

NOPE. NOT GOOD ENOUGH.

YOU SAID YOU WERE READY WHEN YOU CAME HERE.
WE CAN'T JUST LET YOU GO NOW THAT YOU KNOW ABOUT US.
JA (FWK)
STOP.

WE'LL TALK ABOUT THIS LATER.

THE CARRIAGE WILL MOST LIKELY ARRIVE IN YOUR VILLAGE THIS EVENING.
WHEN IT DOES, THEY'LL FIND OUT YOU RAN OFF.

IT'S SAFER FOR YOU TO STAY HERE FOR A FEW DAYS RATHER THAN GOING BACK TO YOUR VILLAGE.
AND...
...IF YOU CHANGE YOUR MIND DURING THAT TIME, SAY SO.
I WON'T FORCE THIS ON YOU. I DON'T WANT TO BRING US DOWN TO THE LEVEL OF THOSE GRAINELIERS.

HOW ABOUT JUST DOING THE TESTS FOR SEED COMPATIBILITY WHILE YOU'RE HERE?
EVEN IF YOU SUDDENLY SAID YOU WANTED TO TAKE A SEED TOMORROW, IT TAKES A LITTLE WHILE TO GET THE RESULTS.

ALL RIGHT.
I'LL DO THAT, THEN.
I HATE TO ADMIT IT, BUT IT'S JUST LIKE YOU'RE BOTH SAYING, HUGUES.
I KNOW I WON'T BE ABLE TO DO ANYTHING IF I GO BACK TO THE VILLAGE LIKE THIS.

AND IT SEEMS LIKE THERE ARE STILL A LOT OF THINGS I DON'T KNOW.
I'LL START BY LEARNING THEM.

LEARNING ABOUT THIS WORLD.

Episode 21

SEEDS AND PEOPLE EACH HAVE TYPES THEY'RE MORE COMPATIBLE WITH.
WE'LL TAKE SOME BLOOD AND NARROW DOWN AS BEST WE CAN WHICH SEEDS WILL BE MOST COMPATIBLE.
SEEDS YOU PLANT DRY UP AND GET DISEASED DEPENDING ON THE SOIL, RIGHT?
SAME THING HERE.
SO I'M THE SOIL?

RIGHT.
IT'S NOT LIKE YOU CAN JUST TAKE ANY POWERFUL SEED YOU WANT.
IT DEPENDS ON THE CONDITION OF THE BODY. PEOPLE VARY IN HOW MUCH OF THE SEED'S POTENTIAL CAN BE HARNESSED.
SOMETIMES, YOU END UP HANDICAPPED BECAUSE OF THE SEED'S TRAITS.

Attaque
ONE EXAMPLE IS EXTREME WEAKNESS IN THE MORNING, MAKING SERIOUS ACTIVITY IMPOSSIBLE. IF YOU'RE ATTACKED BY AN ENEMY IN THE MORNING, YOU'RE MORE LIKELY TO DIE.
YOU HAVE TO CAREFULLY SELECT TRAITS AS WELL FROM THE SEEDS WITH THE HIGHEST POSSIBILITY OF COMPAT-IBILITY.

LUCA—WAS THAT YOUR FRIEND'S NAME?
WHAT KIND OF SEED DOES HE CARRY?
...I DON'T KNOW.

LUCA SAID...
...ONCE, IN THE MIDDLE OF THE NIGHT, OVER A DOZEN GRAINELIERS SUDDENLY CAME TO HIS HOUSE.
BAN (BANG)
THEY SAID THEY WERE LOOKING FOR CHRISTOPHE—LUCA'S FATHER.
CHRIS-TOPHE TOLD LUCA TO EAT THE SEED AND RUN.

SO LUCA'S A CARRIER BECAUSE HE SWALLOWED THE SEED HIS FATHER GAVE HIM?
WHAT ABOUT THE FATHER?
THAT... I DON'T KNOW THAT EITHER.
LUCA'S STILL LOOKING FOR CHRISTOPHE, BUT...

...WHEN I FOUND LUCA ON THE GROUND IN THE VILLAGE, HIS HOUSE WAS ALREADY ON FIRE.
I DON'T KNOW IF CHRISTOPHE IS ALIVE OR DEAD.

AND WITH CHRISTOPHE GONE, WE DON'T KNOW WHAT KIND OF SEED LUCA SWALLOWED.
......
WHY DID THE GRAINELIERS ATTACK? SECRET CULTIVATION IS A SERIOUS CRIME, BUT MORE THAN A DOZEN FROM THE SECURITY FORCE SHOWING UP OUT OF THE BLUE...SEEMS LIKE OVERKILL.
WAS CHRISTOPHE ALSO A CARRIER?
GIVE ME YOUR ARM.
I DON'T KNOW IF CHRISTOPHE WAS A CARRIER OR NOT.

LUCA SAID THERE WAS A ROOM IN THEIR HOUSE LIKE A SEED LAB...
HE SAID CHRISTOPHE WAS DOING ILLEGAL SEED RESEARCH THERE ON HIS OWN.
SECRET CULTIVA-TION, HMM?

CHRIS-TOPHE, HE...
HE'S A FORMER GRAINELIER RESEARCHER.
!

MAKES SENSE...
PUTSU (JAB)

WHAT'S THEIR LAST NAME?
WE SAID LUCA WAS MY RELATIVE, SO HE'S ON THE LIST AS LUCA GUIVARC'H.
BUT HIS REAL NAME IS LUCA ANGLADE.
HIS FATHER'S CHRISTOPHE ANGLADE.
GOT IT. I'LL LOOK INTO IT.
HMM?

WHO'RE YOU?
A- ABEL.
NICE TO MEET YOU.

YOU LOT SAY YOUR NAMES TOO!
RENÉE.
LOÏC...
THOMAS!

IF YOU DON'T RUN, YOU CAN COME IN.
YAY!
OH!
WHERE'D YOU COME FROM?
THE VILLAGE OF NORTOIS.

YOU'RE GETTING SHOTS. I HAA-AATE THEM.
HEY, HUGUES ISN'T PICKING ON YOU, IS HE?
A LITTLE.
REALLY.
I HAAATE HOW HUGUES GETS MAD SO EASY.
HA HA ...
HEY?
ABEL, ARE YOU HUMAN?
OR PLANT?

......
I'M HUMAN.
US TOO!
YOU ARE?
PHEW!
JUST LIKE ME, HUH?

FOR NOW.
ONCE THE SEED SPROUTS, THE PHYSICAL BODY WILL BECOME A PLANT.

AND THEN, IF THEY'VE GOTTEN THE PLANT TRAIT OF LONG LIFE, THEIR GROWTH'LL BECOME EXTREMELY SLOW, SO...
...BY HUMAN STANDARDS, THEY'LL BE CLOSE TO IMMORTAL.
IF YOU DON'T HAVE A CERTAIN LEVEL OF PHYSICAL AND MENTAL DEVELOPMENT WHEN YOU TAKE A SEED, IT'S ACTUALLY DANGEROUS.

WHILE YOU STILL CAN'T CONTROL YOUR OWN FEELINGS, ANYWAY.
THEN...
YES.

THE DAY MIGHT COME WHEN THEY'LL BE CARRIERS TOO.
......
THEY WILL?

BUT I WANNA BE A PLANT RIGHT NOW!
RIGHT, LOÏC!
I-I...
I WANNA BE A PLANT TOO!
HUMANS ARE WEAK. THEY CAN'T DO ANY-THING.
YOU THINK SO TOO, RIGHT, ABEL?

I GUESS SO.
WE CAN'T DO ANY-THING.
WE'LL NEED YOU TO WORK WHILE YOU'RE HERE.
HUH?

EVER COOKED?
S-SOME.

OKAY, LET'S MAKE SOMETHING TOGETHER! I'LL HELP!

ONLY HUMANS EAT HERE.
YOU HAVE TO BE SELF-SUFFICIENT.
HUH?
WHAT?
HURRY! COME ON! HURRY!

WHOA! HOLD ON!
GASHAN (KAKLANG)
NO RUNNING!

FWOO...
FWOO...
FWOO...
Side Story

ガチャー
GACHAN (KACHAK)
AH.
WELCOME HOME.

LUCA...
SORRY. DID I WAKE YOU?
YOU GO ON TO BED.

SIGH.
ARE YOU HUNGRY, DAD?

HMM?
YOU DON'T SEEM VERY HAPPY.
YOU'RE HUNGRY, SO YOU CAN'T BE HAPPY, RIGHT?
HA HA HA!
NO, NO, YOUR DAD'S PLENTY HAPPY.
OH, RIGHT. I BROUGHT YOU SOME-THING.

AN APPLE!
THIS IS AN APPLE FROM A REGION CALLED BEREGNE.
THEY'RE FAMOUS FOR BEING VERY SWEET AND DELI-CIOUS.

IT SMELLS LIKE HONEY.

HA HA!
ALTHOUGH, IT IS THE MIDDLE OF THE NIGHT...
WANT TO EAT ONE WITH YOUR OLD DAD NOW?
MAYBE I'LL CHEER UP IF WE DO.

YEAH.

......
SMELLS SWEET...
ぼー
BO (DAZED)
WAS THAT DREAM BECAUSE OF THIS SMELL?
OH!
LUCA! YOU'RE AWAKE?

...MY BODY HURTS.
GISHI (KRRK)
WAS I ASLEEP AGAIN?
YUP.
I GUESS YOU WERE ASLEEP ABOUT TWO WEEKS?
IT'S BECAUSE IT'S GOTTEN COLDER LATELY.
WINTER'S LIKE YOUR HIBER-NATING PERIOD, HUH?
APPLES.
A WHOLE PILE OF THEM.
OH, RIGHT. RIGHT.
MY AUNT GIVES US SOME EVERY YEAR. SHE LIVES IN THE NEXT TOWN OVER, BEREGNE.
SHE'S AN APPLE FARMER, SO...

THEY HAD A BUMPER CROP, SO WE GOT A LOT THIS YEAR.
I WAS GONNA MAKE JAM OUT OF THEM BEFORE THEY GO BAD.

HMM?
YOU'RE HAVING AN APPLE?
YOU DIDN'T WANT ANY FOOD, THOUGH?

I'M NOT GOING TO EAT IT.
BUT THIS SMELL...
I STILL LIKE IT QUITE A BIT.
...HUH.
OKAY, THEN. HELP ME PEEL THEM!
THERE'S STILL A TON TO GET THROUGH.
GRAINELIERS 2 END

Next time...

MY BODY, A PLANT...
ME?
AND TO BEGIN WITH, IS LUCA REALLY A SEED CARRIER?
Abel struggles with whether he should accept power...
...from the anti-Grainelier forces...
NO, I CAN'T DO ANYTHING ABOUT THAT RIGHT NOW, NO MATTER HOW HARD I THINK ABOUT IT.
THE FACT IS I NEED POWER TO RESCUE LUCA.

...when he encounters a mysterious boy...

...and is tossed toward the center of the fight.

Graineliers Volume 3 — Coming Soon!

GRAINELIERS

thanks a lot!

WE'VE SOMEHOW MADE IT TO THE PUBLICATION OF VOLUME 2. I'M SORRY TO HAVE KEPT YOU WAITING... WE'LL CONTINUE A LITTLE LONGER, SO IF YOU'RE ENJOYING IT, I'D BE DELIGHTED IF YOU'D JOIN US IN THE NEXT VOLUME TOO.

RIHITO TAKARAI

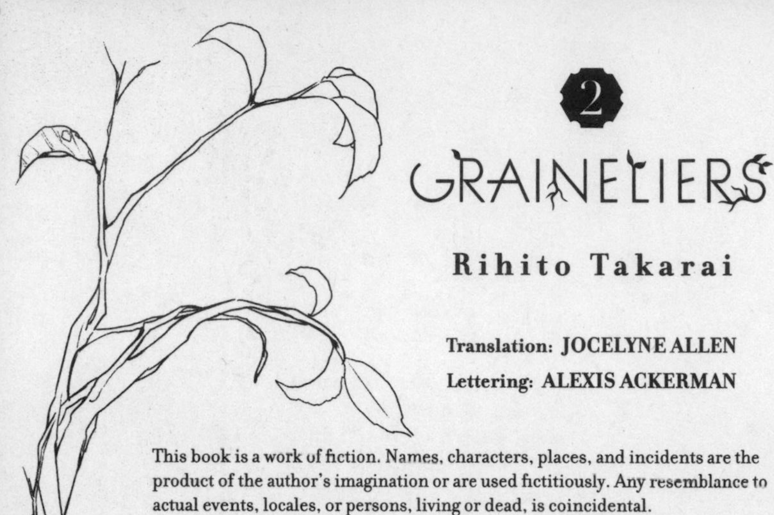

GRAINELIERS 2

Rihito Takarai

Translation: JOCELYNE ALLEN
Lettering: ALEXIS ACKERMAN

Yen Press
1290 Avenue of the Americas
New York, NY 10104

Visit us at yenpress.com
facebook.com/yenpress
twitter.com/yenpress
yenpress.tumblr.com
instagram.com/yenpress

First Yen Press Edition: February 2018

Yen Press is an imprint of Yen Press, LLC.
The Yen Press name and logo are trademarks of Yen Press, LLC.

The publisher is not responsible for websites (or their content) that are not owned by the publisher.

Library of Congress Control Number: 2017949554

ISBNs: 978-0-316-41599-6 (paperback)
978-0-316-44840-6 (ebook)

10 9 8 7 6 5 4 3 2 1

BVG

Printed in the United States of America